All In: A Novel of Love in Poetry is a brilliant and seamless look at the way two lives become one. Written like a novel in two voices the book eventually blends until the voices are one voice telling a story about time, survival and love. In a very real way we see how these people reconnect and overcome trauma that had kept them apart. This is a real look at the small but oh so important moments that make a relationship last and a love grow deeper over time. As a sailor who deployed in 2020 to Manhattan to work in a make-shift hospital, I found the Covid experience shared here rang true and the details important and very real. Also as a man married for 27 years, I believe I know real love when I see it. I rooted for Sarah and Norman from the start and I felt each small beautiful thing that happened to both of them!!
--Matthew Borczon, retired Navy Hospital Corpsman, author of 19 books of poetry, including *Post Deployment.*

All In, written by Pris Campbell and Scott Owens, is a sequel to their book *Shadows Trail Them Home*, featuring Sara and Norman who reunite so many years later. Like other readers enraptured by the original story, I have waited for another collaboration. These well-crafted poems exemplify all the honed skills you'd expect from these talented poets, with a call-and-response feel between the two main characters' poems and a compelling narrative that had me turning pages to see what happened next. Even the *Afterwords* is brilliant and offers a glimpse of their writing process, their alter egos, and their long-lasting friendship. This was the book I didn't know I needed to read. Norman says in one of the poems, "he has fallen in love with happy endings," to which I must respond, "Me, too, Norman. Me, too."
--Malaika King Albrecht, Heart of Pamlico Poet Laureate

I've long been a fan of Pris Campbell's work and am delighted to have discovered her collaborating with the wonderfully talented Scott Owens in this book. These two make quite a pair. Their poetic acumen is matched in this book by their depth of empathy for their characters, Norman and Sara, a neat trick indeed. The poems combine into a seamless narrative as remarkable as the story they tell. This is a book of great power with its deep dive into the territories of love, lust, sickness, loss and redemption. The reader becomes a voyeur to the stripped bare needs – both the beautiful and the mundane -- of these all-too-human characters. Prepare yourself for an intimate journey that will leave you sometimes breathless, sometimes broken, always engaged, always wanting more.
--Jeff Weddle, author of *Driving the Lost Highway.*

Also by Pris Campbell and Scott Owens

The Nature of Attraction
Shadows Trail Them Home

Also by Pris Campbell

Truth and Other Lies
My Southern Childhood
Squall Line on the Horizon
When the Wolves Come after You Hang On (with Michael Parker)
Postscripts to the Dead
Paul Newman Blues
Sea Trails
Hesitant Commitments
Abrasions
Interchangeable Goddesses (with Tammy Trendle)

Also by Scott Owens

Prepositional
Worlds Enough: Poems for Children (with Missy Cleveland)
Sky Full of Stars and Dreaming
Counting the Ways
Down to Sleep
Thinking about the Next Big Bang in the Galaxy at the Edge of Town
To
Eye of the Beholder
For One Who Knows How to Own Land
Country Roads: Travels through Rural North Carolina
Something Knows the Moment
Paternity
The Fractured World
Book of Days
Deceptively Like a Sound
The Persistence of Faith

ALL IN

A NOVEL OF LOVE IN POETRY

SEQUEL TO *SHADOWS TRAIL THEM HOME*

By Pris Campbell & Scott Owens

REDHAWK
PUBLICATIONS

Redhawk Publications
The Catawba Valley Community College Press
2550 US Hwy 70 SE
Hickory NC 28602

ISBN: 978-1-959346-12-8

Library of Congress Number: 2023938755

Printed in the United States of America

redhawkpublications.com

Cover Design & Layout By: Ashlyn Blake

Cover Photo By: Pris Campbell

Contents

Epilogue

Prologue

Recognizing the Moment

Palm Court Inn & Suites

Alive and Growing

Better

Consummation

Afterwords

EPILOGUE

. . . when they thought it was over

Potholes

Sara stumbles across Norman's latest book,
has stopped googling his name,
avoids poetry readings,
but there it sits on a site she rarely visits,
as if it were a pothole
waiting for her to trip over.

She can't catch her breath,
her heart already running
across the street leaving behind
this pale, frozen ghost of a woman,
to deal with feelings she was certain
she had placed in an attic somewhere.

Now she remembers the hint
of mint when he kissed her,
his clothes always folded just so
on the chair before the other Norman
came out to carry her up mountains
she'd never climbed with other men
when he came inside her, night
after night, sometimes all night.

She wonders if he ever runs across
one of her paintings in a gallery
and loses his breath, too, his heart
galloping down the street like hers,
wonders what it would be like
if he'd had the courage to stay
with her and the boy, to let go
of the walls he built stone by stone
around himself, fearing that one day
the castle would collapse
and he would lie there
in the rubble, unable to deal with fists
that still had the urge to strike out,
unable to ward off memories of a childhood
that branded him too deeply to risk
what he might do to his own boy, to her.

Sinkholes

Not his breath, but his way,
and not stumbling, but seeking them out,
almost every day, after the job,
and the bills, the daily duties,
when the loneliness starts to set in.
Sometimes he goes to the bar
or the bottle, but mostly he goes
to the gallery, one or another
where he knows he'll find it,
a world to get lost in, again,
standing for hours, staring
at the paints, yes, but seeing
memory or what might have been,
and losing, yes, sense of time,
place, purpose, hope, but not his breath,
the one thing that stays caught,
for better or worse, the paradox
of being lost in what he's lost.

PROLOGUE

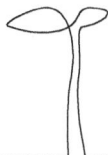

Flashback: Sara's Prologue

Sara wakes up sweating.
The dream was so real.
A young Norman
making love to her again.
Norman fearful from his own
childhood abuse that he
would be like his father
and hit the boy or her.

Norman leaving in a rush,
not coming back, his fears
overtaking him. Norman hiding
at the street corner for years
thinking she didn't see him
but she did and made sure
the boy was dressed nicely,
hair long but cut neatly, a smile
on his face from a joke she told.

Sara thinks of her own childhood
molestation, the way she went through men
like they were expendable,
screwing them all to prove something,
to live up to grandpa's words,
You little whore, when he touched her
in forbidden places.

Then Norman came along.
From the beginning he felt like
her soul twin. She wanted no-one else
but him. But he left. Part of her was lost
with him but she was determined.
No man would ever destroy her again
and so she survived.

Not happily like with Norman
but she's always known happiness
is a game played with melting pawns.

Norman's Prologue

The curse of his father made him avoid relationships
for years, one night stands were fine, even
a week or two, maybe a month at most.
But when things got serious, he would find a way to leave
or make them want to. He put all that aside
for Sara. And thought he was finally past his childhood
until a child of his own came along and taught him
he wasn't. It left him completely broken to leave,
but having lost it once, he was fully convinced
that going was better than repeating on Sara and the boy
what had been done to him. He moved away,
went back to his old ways, writing poetry,
remodeling the house he got for nothing,
at the Sound-end of a long, dirt road,
bringing home women from readings
and bars as needed, those impressed with how
he wrote, spoke, looked, all the usual
ways a man appealed to a woman, but none of them
ever reached as deep as Sara. He heard
from her now and then, letting him know
about the boy. He even went south several times
to see for himself, wondering if he'd made the right
decision, wondering how he could make it up to the boy,
wondering if she might ever take him back,
wondering if he could ever be worth forgiving.

RECOGNIZING THE MOMENT

Sara's Fate

Sara has finally decided
hope for Norman is long gone.
The man she lived with after him,
but never would marry,
is dead now— hit and run cancer.

She said yes when this new man
asked her to live with him, a man
who reminded her of Norman
in the almost obsessive way
he folded his clothes,
placed his knife and fork just so.

He didn't make love like Norman
but she had hoped one day
she would lose herself in his arms.
In every other way he pleased her.

But now, after Covid segueing
into long term Covid she's weak
all the time. Some days
she can't get up. Her mind is muddled.
Her paint brushes lie untouched.

He starts screaming at her
(had started three months before)
but brings her soup and crackers,
drives her to the doctor.
Still, his rage attacks bounce off the walls.
Stunned, she wants to leave but can barely
pull on a tee shirt and jeans,
much less untwine the twining
of their things done earlier,
or unlease her old place to return.

She covers her ears, blocks out the light,
pretends she's dancing in the park again,
chalking purple breasts on the sidewalk.
She pretends the boy, Norman's son,
young again, runs behind her, flowers
opening in their passing.

If she could endure Norman's leaving,
she can endure anything,
she tells herself. Even the crazy man
storming about in the living room.

Norman's Dream

Footsteps on the pavement alert him—
but no, it's not the kid he paid
to fill a bag with stones, twigs,
golden leaves.

He's building an effigy
to lure his muse. It grows
more complex each day
but to no avail.

He could write for Hallmark,
given the nonsense that flows
these days from his useless pen.
Dark skies, black clouds
hover, just to rain on him.
Restless, he dozes at last.

He feels someone with him . . .
the boy, back in the night?
No, not the boy,
but her— the old love he's not seen
in years, that daring woman
who danced topless
in their apartment window,
painted purple breasts
on sidewalks and canvas,
held a lamp to his darkness.

She's older now
Grey streaks run through her hair,
But she's still slender, tiny breasts
taut against her blouse.
He shakes inside.

The weather is nice.
Are you still painting?
Care for some tea?
He tries to find words.

She touches his shoulder,
leans up for an unexpected kiss.
The wildness of their past passion
returns, his muse singing,
clouds rushing away.

Forget the stones, the leaves.
He enters that place he's longed
to return to for so long, but was afraid.

They write poems of a different kind
until he wakes.

A Man Less Broken

A man less broken might not have answered
when she called not having heard from her
since the boy left home,
10 years of self-imposed silence.

A man less broken might not have driven
all night 12 hours down dark deserted
roads alone remembering
all the things he'd wanted to be.

A man less broken might have called
the police, might have sent the boy
to tell her she deserved better, to offer
to help her get help, to offer
to help her get out.

A man less broken might have spoken
before striking out when the door opened,
might have asked for explanation,
understanding, patience.

A man less broken might have known
it wasn't just the man before him
he struck again and again and again
but that part of himself that made him leave,
that part of himself his father gave him.

A man less broken would have stopped
before she appeared on the stairs,
her face a confusion of hope and horror
but still the face of someone he cared for
more than himself, and in that moment

he saw, at last, no memories of pain,
anger, fear, no memories of his father,
no memories of anything but her,
and he knew, even a man this broken
might find a way to trust
himself enough to stay.

Caught Off Guard

Never one to be surprised,
shocked, caught off guard,
Norman thought he was prepared
for anything, but he never expected
time to stand still, everything
fall away to silence,
all his senses to deaden
to anything that wasn't her.

He knew he had never stopped
loving her, he knew his emotions
would swell when he saw her,
but he never imagined his breath,
mind, motion, very being
would catch when she appeared.
He never imagined that what she thought
of who he was still mattered
more than anything else to him.

Recognizing the Moment

Imagine the fisherman who thought he saw
something strange on the horizon for 12 seconds
near Kitty Hawk on December 17, 1903.
Imagine the shepherd watching Moses
talking to a bush set on fire.
What a loon! he must have thought.
Imagine the attendant who opened the doors
to the Curia Pompey for 40 senators
on March 15 in the year 44.

Norman was not like any of these
as he stood at the bottom of the stairs.
He knew the importance of this moment.

He had first stopped breathing
when he saw her, and he stepped back
to see better and let her see him.
He found he could move no further though,
and stood as still as a shirt on a rack,
being judged, decided upon, whether to put on
or put back. He hadn't thought about what
he would say, and now no words came to him,
but he knew that everything he had ever wanted,
everything he had hoped could somehow be,
his future, his wholeness, his very life,
hung in the balance of that moment.

Questions

She never thought he would come.
She had called him on impulse,
pretending it was about the boy,
expecting him not to answer.
She found herself spilling the story,
unexpectedly, then asking for ideas
about where she could go,
who could help her. And now,
there he is just inside her doorway,
huge hands around the throat
of the man she lives with,
pinned against the wall,
face bleeding, and Norman yelling,
If you ever hurt her again,
I'll kill you.

When he sees her,
he stops, his face
softens, and he lets go,
steps back.

The man moves towards the door,
unnoticed, glances up at Sara,
sees truth in her eyes
and says, *You want her.*
You got her.
I'll come back when she's gone.
Get her stuff out of my house!

Still caught in Norman's stare,
mind racing, heart pounding,
breath held, Sara feels faint,
finally retreats to her room,
afraid to see him, afraid
she had imagined the look
in his eyes, imagined him at all.

She falls back on the side of the bed,
waiting to know what to do next.
He follows, enters slowly,
kneels before her. His hair
as silver as hers now, his face
thinner, but still no stubble
clinging to his cheeks.
She takes it all in. He remains
as silent as she, both afraid
to break the spell, say the first word.

At last, she reaches out her hand.
After a pause, he covers it with his.

Aftermath

Norman suggests a hotel,
in case the man comes back,
separate rooms, a communicating door.
Sara agrees.
He says he'll get a storage unit,
call movers if she can label what goes.
Sara agrees,
says she doesn't care
about most of it,
asks if he needs to eat.
He says no, apologizes.
She is quiet.
He asks if she can get around okay.
She thinks so.
He rises to begin making the calls,
forgets to let go of her hand.
She does too.

Packing It In

She doesn't have much to pack,
her place was rented furnished.
No room to move much in here.
Just her favorite rocking chair,
clothes, books and art supplies,
the usual day to day things
a person needs. A box of photos
is in a dresser drawer, mostly
of the boy when he was growing up,
some with Norman before he left.
She keeps those at the bottom,
unable to look at them again.

A beat up copy of *Persuasion*,
her favorite, and very unlike
her Wild Woman artist image,
tops a pile of books. She could
relate to the feeling that the man
the heroine loved might never
love her again.

Her paintings are most important.
She brought the unsold ones
not in galleries with her.
She wonders if Norman
noticed the one painting,
her very favorite, an abstract
of Norman, hands cupping
the breasts of a purple breasted
woman, one leg thrust between
her thighs. She had painted
it one night in a sexual frenzy
for him not long after he left.
Many offers had been made
for it but that was one she
would never sell.

She points things out to Norman
then collapses, exhausted
from trying to make sure she has it all.
She never wants to return here again.

What He Didn't Know

It would be impossible to say
what went into his decision.
Norman wasn't sure it even counted
as a decision, more an intuition,
instinct. The plan, if it could be called
that, seemed to come together
all at once as he stood at the bottom
of the stairs looking up at her.

He had known for years
that he was over his past.
He had known that he still cared.
He had known she would still be beautiful,
and he would still want her. He had known
he still loved her. What he didn't know
was how much, how much she needed him,
how much he needed to be needed.

And he didn't know how to make
this happen, only that he had to.

Leaving

While she sleeps, Norman packs
a suitcase with things she'll need now,
points out things to be boxed
to the man whose name Sara gave him
for his skill at safely crating paintings,
Norman carefully labeling after him.
He found an air conditioned unit
plenty big enough and necessary
for the paintings.

When all is done, the truck packed
and gone, Norman sets the house key out,
carries Sara to his car
with a gentleness unexpressed
for years, now weightless in his arms.

PALM COURT INN & SUITES

Checking In

Sara wakes alone,
a vase of white tulips
on the nightstand, a note
propped against them,
Going to get breakfast and supplies.
Found someone to help get your car.
Back soon.
(She's glad of that).
Just text if you need me sooner.
Sara had walked in
but could manage little else
the night before.

Norman has left everything
laid out so it is easy to find.
The communicating door is open.
She pulls herself up
and carefully explores the rooms,
nice enough for one night
but nowhere you'd want to stay for long.
Each has identical nightstands,
chests of drawers, desks with wheeled chairs,
and double beds. His is already made
or perhaps undisturbed.
She remembers how the nightmares
plagued him. She wonders
if he slept at all.

She decides to shower,
a risky move in her condition,
but she's determined.
When she reappears
he is ready to help her.
The desk is moved to the window
and turned into a table,
both chairs next to it,
strawberry and cream croissants,
fresh plums, granola,
hot coffee waiting.

He tells her other groceries
are in the chest of drawers,
apples, bananas, bread,
peanut butter, paper goods,
a few cans that can
be heated in the microwave.
He says the manager will bring
a mini-fridge later today.
And tea. He remembered
she likes tea, but couldn't remember
which one, so he brought chamomile,
red berries, strawberry oolong, elderberry,
Moroccan mint, English breakfast,
and vanilla caramel chai.

He opens the curtains and they sit
in the sun and eat and chat
for hours about health, and homes,
and work, and the boy, and lost time.
When they are done, she says
she needs to rest. He suggests
she put his number on speed dial.
She says it always has been.

Catching It

Sara's pretty sure she knows
where she got it, not that it matters now.
The art gallery downtown wanted
a photo next to one of her art pieces
displayed in the front window.

She went early since she would have to
take off her mask. Others might go
without them, but she was careful,
wearing hers even when people stared.

The owner introduced her to the photographer
and went back to his office while they worked.
The photographer wore no mask, refused
the one Sara offered him, *It gets in my way,* he said.
He coughed several times, blaming it on allergies.

Four days later, Sara's throat was sore.
Her chest felt tight. The next day she tested
positive, quarantining herself in a spare room
at the new man's house.

She had already realized he was a mistake,
was trying to find a place to live again
when she got sick. How dumb, she told herself,
both about the man and the photographer.
Though she didn't have to tell herself. The new man
had already been telling her through the door
off and on all day, more pissed they couldn't
have sex than worried about her illness.

What Sara Doesn't Know

Sara doesn't know how much better she'll get,
if she'll get better at all. The doctors can tell her nothing.

Sara doesn't know if Norman will change his mind
being around a sick woman. So much helping out.
It's exhausting.

Sara doesn't know if she can make love the way
she used to. She wants to, already lusts for Norman's
way of doing things. Lusts for Norman however he does it.
She never thought she would feel that again.

Sara doesn't know if he'll leave again.
The scariest thought of all.

Sara to the Boy

Their second day in Palm Court Inn & Suites,
her mind finally clear enough,
she texts the boy to tell him
where she is, what's happened.
She doesn't tell him about Norman yet.
She needs time to find the best way
to tell him he is back after all this time,
to tell him it is good.

She isn't sure yet what
would happen between them, needs time
to sort that out before getting the boy
hopeful. Despite how quickly Norman left,
the boy had hoped for years he would
return to them, even after John moved
in with them and did things a father
would do with him — he wasn't his father.

Sara gave the boy a couple of photos
of Norman holding him when he was small.
She relented when he told her he could
barely remember his face anymore.
He had the photos framed and displayed
where he lived, four hours away,
with his wife and young son.

The boy had wanted to come when she got sick
but it wasn't safe then and later, she told him
to come when his work wasn't so busy.
He argued but finally agreed.

Yes, she needs to prepare him
for what he had wanted so long ago.

Norman Knew

Norman knew there was much to be done.
He also knew Sara needed
to get out. He convinced her to go for a ride
around town just to *Get some sun
and fresh air and let housekeeping
do their work.* They drove almost aimlessly
around, Norman silently looking
at neighborhoods, watching and listening
to where Sara seemed most interested,
thinking about where she might like to live.
They went downtown and Norman pushed
Sara through the open air market
for nearly an hour, stopping to chat
with vendors, gather produce,
look at crafts. They ended up at a park
nearby and Norman pulled a blanket
from the trunk so they could lie in the sun.
She fell asleep with her head in his lap.
While she slept he did what he had been doing
for days, making calls, writing texts,
keeping things quietly moving forward.

Keeping Watch

Sara wakes to the sound of whistling
from the shower, *I'll Stand By You.*
She knows it's Norman.
She knows, too, that she's still dressed.
She remembers a rough spell the night before,
blinding headache, exhaustion,
impossible to move. She had pushed
herself too much yesterday but didn't
regret it. She'd asked him to hold her.
He made her feel warm, safe,
helped her relax, until she fell asleep.
She sees the extra blanket
neatly folded on the chair,
knows he likely stayed there
all night, just watching.
She rises quietly, glides
to the bathroom door, decides
to do a little watching of her own.

Palm Court Inn & Suites

The two rooms, the absence
of room to cook, have become
untenable, and after yesterday
unnecessary. The manager says
they can have a suite at the end
of the week. Sara imagines
she'll like sharing a bed,
a shower, not feeling a need
to be always dressed. She's already
noticed how he looks at her,
when she walks, eyes hungry,
always stopping
at least a moment to admire.
She'd like more of that.

Pretty In Pink

Now moved into the suite of rooms,
Sara is having a stronger day.
While Norman steps out for food
she climbs onto the shower seat
he bought her, scrubs her body
in warm water and pulls
on her favorite pink nightshirt,
the one that flatters. He hasn't seen
her body. Her breasts have fallen,
muscles untoned from her weakness.

When he opens the door he looks
at her and she knows her body will be
okay . . . they won't delay any longer.
She may not be the Energizer bunny
in bed like before but she's already damp
from wanting him.

He hurriedly puts the food in the kitchenette fridge
and comes to her, unbuttoning his shirt,
pulling off his trousers and folding them neatly
over the chair in his old Norman way.
He could be the young Norman again,
this time their first time.

Her nightshirt off they lie body to body.
She doesn't have to tell him how to please her
like the others. His hands and mouth go
to the right spots, as hers do with him.
When she can no longer stand it, she pulls
him inside her. Nothing has changed.
Her head whirls with the ecstasy.
Soon, too soon, she spasms
and they do it all over again a short rest later.
She sleeps curled in his arms, waking
to find herself reaching for him again.

Finally she sleeps. He curls next to her,
dinner long forgotten.

Norman Does Laundry

Like most laundromats it's not anywhere
you'd want to stay long, the smell of age
and mold masked only by detergent
and bleach. Fully half the fluorescents
flicker or don't work at all. And the other
patrons are a collection that could hardly
earn even the term, *ragtag*:
coed wearing less clothing than she should,
texting, taking selfies with her legs spread;
overweight, middle aged, balding man
in clothes still too big for him surrounded
on hard plastic seats by every variety
of chips and chocolate the vend-o-mat has;
a couple with disarrayed hair and no clothes
to wash besides what they wear
pumping coins into the Jackpot 6000
and swearing every time they come up empty.
Good character material, Norman might normally
say, but today his focus is entirely on the task
before him. Handling Sara's clothes
makes him think of her. He treats each piece
as gently as if he were touching her. He lingers
probably more than he should in a public place
on each one, insuring he bags the delicates
to protect them, sorting by color and material,
and using just enough organic, scent-free cleanser
to make things clean without wearing them out.
While he waits and watches, his mind wanders
over past and future, how to get farther from one,

how to keep moving closer to the other.
He leaves feeling clearer than he has in years.

What Next

They moved to the suite two weeks ago.
It gives them more room but still
not enough. A stop gap solution at best.
Sara is getting used to sleeping with Norman,
the warmth of his body, his sounds in the night.
Sharing meals with him is special, too.
A tiny dinette came with the suite and he cooks
their meals for now. She hopes she can get
back to it but their tastes are similar. They both
like fresh salads and vegetables, a bit of fish
or chicken. Neither are greasy spoon types.
He cleans up after meals, too, and makes their bed.
He's already gone to the laundromat twice.

Norman hasn't said anything about what
he wants to do next. Will he set her up there
until her tenants' lease expires in two months,
come to visit her, staying part of the time.
In her heart she senses he loves her
though neither has used the word.
Maybe it's the off and on headaches,
the weakness getting her down some days
but she fears this is a dream too good to be true.

The Boy Insists

The boy has checked in with her
almost daily and now won't take no
for an answer. He's taking a three day
weekend and coming to help her.
He has a friend he can stay with overnight.

He has no way yet of knowing
Norman is there to help her, thinks
she's struggling all alone, paying people
to bring food in, to bring everything she needs.
He insists she must break
the lease – she can't stay where she is
for two months. They'll understand.
He's met them and knows they're caring people.

Time to tell him the truth.
Slowly she tells him Norman is with her,
how he helped her get away from the jerk,
found this place, got her things stored,
is making sure she eats and rests.
She tells him how strongly she feels for Norman,
wants him in her life again, his fears
that took him away earlier seem almost overcome.

The boy is silent. At first she thinks he's afraid
it won't work, that Norman will run again.
Finally she realizes something in the tone
of her voice has convinced him that things
are different between them this time.
She knows because he says,
Dad is back?

Reassured that she's not alone
and probably needs time with Norman,
he tells her he'll come later, admitting
Yes, work is a zoo. She knows he wants
to see Norman badly but also knows
they need time to rebuild.

When the Memory's Too Much

Sara wakes to music
from the unit next door.
She reaches out to touch Norman.
Our Song! she whispers.
The music flows through her head,
nudging synapses with memories
of their first days...
holding hands, making love,
becoming besotted with each other,
this song ever in the background.

She should have gone after him
when he first left, dragged him back,
tied him up to make him stay.

Norman is already kissing her.
She can see the universe
expand in his eyes.

Norman Sells His House

Norman sells his house in no time.
He had gotten it for almost nothing,
worked on it for years. He stayed
close by to Sara and the boy, at first,
to catch occasional glances, but when
a new man moved in he knew
he had to get away as far as possible.
Next to poetry, the new house became
his passion, certainly his distraction.
Soundfront, updated, immaculate now,
it brings a tidy profit. He arranges
to have only books and papers,
a few artifacts, sent down,
has the rest sold,
tells Sara, *I'm all in.*

Second Chances

Things rarely come out right
the first time. We screw, unscrew,
rescrew to get it straight. We measure,
cut, measure again, curse a little,
make it plumb. We miss turns,
bend the nail, plant the bulbs
upside down, burn the bread,
change clothes, regret the faux pas,
Freudian slip, hasty decision.
Who among us has never needed
to apologize for the poorly timed
comment, unwitting offensive joke?
We hope we learn from each attempt
what we need to do it better
the next time. We hope we learn enough
to deserve a second chance, enough
to find a way to forgive ourselves.

What Changed

They're both older.
Maybe they expect less.
Maybe they're more patient,
their schedules less demanding.
Maybe they love themselves more.

Norman knows the world
will never be the way
he sees it in his head,
has learned the effort
is its own reward,
has let go of the past.

Some things are the same.
He never stopped loving her.
She still leaves him speechless.
He still wants it all to be just right,
but now, more than anything else
in his mind, she needs him
to be the man he should be.

Sara Tells Her Secret

She's never told Norman about her success
with her art work. The sale of her paintings
has been enough over the past ten years
that she could stop her odd jobs here and there,
only offering workshops or individual lessons
for the fun of it. The money was enough
for her to almost completely pay for her studio
and living quarters now with some left over
to live modestly on along with the rent.

A gay married art couple are the renters,
tell her time after time how much they love it,
how it feels like home, how they would buy it
in a second if she ever decides to sell.
She's been dreading telling them they will have to leave.

She knows Norman has done well with his poetry, too,
both teaching and selling his books. He's still
an attractive man. She imagines he's had his share
of groupies, wonders if he's made love a lot.
Why should it bother her? She's been with her last
long term man, though not in love, and now,
the jerk who fooled her with his smooth ways.
She'll tell Norman about the money,
hopes it'll be okay.

Saying it First

Neither of them had used the love word yet,
though, in truth, Sara knew she had never
stopped loving him. She knew now that he
still loved her, too, but she was afraid
to say it first. What if it scared him.
What if he wanted this but not more.

He had gone out to run errands again.
The fridge in the suite didn't hold much.
When he returned he was quieter than usual,
disappeared into the bathroom for a long time.
When he came out he looked pale. Nervous.
Asked her to come sit by him on the bed.

She feared he had decided this was too much
to handle. Instead, he pulled out a small box,
took out a ring with a purple stone rimmed
in silver, slipped it onto her finger. I love you
and will always love you, he said.
Think of me when you wear it.

She threw herself into his arms.
I love you, too, she told him, pulling his mouth
down to hers. Hearts joined,
their bodies came next.

Counting the Years

He spent 20 years fearing others,
another 10 fearing himself,
20 more fearing he could never
be forgiven the damage he'd done,
never forgive himself.
Those who talk of second chances
might say *he's too old to try again,*
maybe it's not worth the risk, the effort.
How many good years can you expect?
He can't count how many he's wasted,
but he feels younger than ever
and filled with purpose. In a sense
time has lost its meaning, as if
each day opens for its own sake,
and even one like this would be worth it.

More Sales

When Sara first got Covid
she asked the boy to check
her business email for any sales
by the gallery and auction house
where she had placed her paintings.
The boy's name was on her business
checking account and whenever
she placed her art the seller
was authorized to send a check
to the boy if Sara was unavailable.

She took out her laptop, now online
again, and was pleased to see that several
of her larger paintings had sold.
More money to share with Norman
for their expenses.

She had started out on small sales sites
but as her art became known, collectors
came looking for her. She only painted
when the urge hit her — those were always
her best work. Now she felt ready to start
another painting. Being with Norman
had freed up her emotions and she wanted
them down on canvas.

Atonement

On bad days, the two rooms
had been almost impossible.
He'd carry her everywhere,
just no room for a chair
to work. The suite
was only a little better.
So he looked for a house
with no step-ups or step-downs,
with wide doorways,
and level access to outside.
He found it, a half-mile
from downtown, small
backyard surrounded by sweetbay
and lower plants all around.
A bungalow, so he knew
he could make guest quarters
upstairs. She planned
on having the boy to visit,
a thought that terrified Norman.
Even a roll-in shower
with sliding doors,
and a big front room
with lots of light and a view
of the street. She wouldn't be able
to go out the front door
but she could enter and exit
from the drive and the backyard
straight into the kitchen.
He used the money from selling

his house on Roanoke
but needed her signature
to put her name
next to his on the deed.
When he asked her,
she sat still, staring,
a moment, not understanding
why. He only said, *The boy*.
Then tears fell from both
their eyes and they hugged
as she spoke and breathed
an exhalation of relief
in a single utterance of, *Yes*.

The Renters

Sara calls Mary, the older of the two renters,
says, *If you still want to buy it's yours.*
She hears Mary scream to her partner,
We can stay.

Home values have gone way up since she bought,
but she wants to be fair, so they discuss prices.
Mary inherited money from her mother
but they had never found the cozy, well lit place
they found with Sara. Mary says they can pay
the price Sara settles on. All that's left to do
is set up inspections, get a mortgage
for the part they don't have and a closing
should be possible in the near future.
Mary screams again, sends Sara a virtual hug.

Sara can barely wait to tell Norman that they'll have
a considerable sum of money even after she pays off
her remaining mortgage, her gift to their ongoing
relationship, and a bit of balance for the house.

ALIVE AND GROWING

Studio

The new house has a well-lit room,
large and unneeded,
that Sara declares will be her studio.
Norman gets her paints out of storage
even before the furniture.
She has new canvases delivered.
She starts small but quickly
ramps up to a canvas
nearly the size of a wall.
She paints as long as she can,
first on her feet, then sitting,
sometimes even lying down.

One day he comes in to find her
propped up on her elbows
painting the beach in front
of an ocean so large it seems
he could swim into it if he wanted.
He lies down beside her and watches.
Without a word she begins painting
his face, then rolls him over,
opens his shirt to paint
his chest, then has him press
it against the canvas. She stands
to look at it, and he unbuttons
her blouse, dips his hands
in purple paint, gently rubs
it on each breast. She presses them
next to his on the canvas,

then tells him to lie down
and climbs on top of him,
and they make love imagining
the sounds of gulls above them.

Sharing the Money

Norman has money left over
even after he bought the house.
He makes more on his books,
his reputation growing
and he still has the trust his aunt
left him, so he's not worried,
but Sara insists her house sales
money go into both their names.

It's only fair, she argues.

He doesn't care about fair, he says.
He only wants her to be okay,
and the boy. He finally persuades her
to put it in an irrevocable trust.
For the boy, he tells her,

but she's stubborn.
Half to the boy.
Half to Norman.

Okay, he says. *In my will
it has always been set
for the two of you anyway.*

Norman Acts Like He's 20

Norman acts like he's 20 again.
He whistles all the time,
Ode to Joy,
Can't Take My Eyes Off of You,
Make You Feel My Love,
rushes around writing
scraps of poetry everywhere,
does things no man his age should,
climbs ladders, patches the roof,
carries loads up and down the stairs,
digs in the garden even in the heat of day,
works at making things right
for hours on end,
seems tireless, even in bed.
Sara worries he feels he has to.
He replies *It's always and only that he wants to.*

Doc Time

It's time for Sara's two month
check up in the clinic about half
an hour away, so Norman drives her.
Masks are required, of course.
Sara has plenty of the KN95s,
but so does Norman. He stocked up
as soon as he and Sara moved
to Palm Court. He has alcohol
spray, too, for cleaning faucet handles
and door knobs, and hand cleaner
for when they touch things
away from the house.

The doctor is pleased to hear she's moved out
from the other man. His sarcastic,
disbelieving comments weren't made
just when they were alone.
Try to keep your stress down, he had told her
before, explaining that it changed cortisol
levels in the body and exacerbated symptoms
of fatigue when they fluctuated and dropped
too far. He made clear back then, staring at the other man,
that stress didn't cause long term Covid. Nobody
knew yet why some people got it and others didn't.

 He checks over the vitals the nurse had taken,
then listens to her lungs and checks her throat again.

When finished, he asks about her energy,
memory, dizziness, breathing, balance,
headaches– all symptoms she still had
when she last saw him.

She tells him they still come and go, but she
has someone helping her now, indicating Norman,
who is impressed with how thorough
the doctor is. Had he been lacking, Norman
would have looked for someone better.

The doctor clears his throat and says
he doesn't want to embarrass if she prefers
not discussing it in front of Norman,
but last time she said she had also lost her sex drive,
was unable to have sex with the man
she was living with due also to weakness.
(*Not just weakness*, Sara thinks to herself).

He asks if that has changed.
Norman and Sara look at each other
and laugh. *Not a problem with the sex drive*,
she tells him. No dummy, the doctor
chuckles too. Sara adds, *I still have times
when I'm too weak or have the bad headaches,
but the desire is back.*

He gives her the antibodies script, as well as one
to check her liver enzymes, reminds her
again to pace her energy, rest, and eat well.
In a few months if things are the same
he wants another immunological workup
for the basics. Their institute has a research grant
from NIH now. She could be a part of if need be.

His secretary will call if she needs
to come back sooner than two months
or get a booster, based on the bloodwork.
They leave hand in hand. Norman picks up
a flier on the research grant the doctor mentioned
on their way out. He brings the car around
and helps her get comfortable in the seat,
hand caressing her shoulder.

Sara Remembers

Sara remembers
and the first day she has the strength
to cook in her new kitchen
she makes deviled eggs,
pimientos shaped into hearts
on top, and potato salad
with caramelized onions
and fried bacon. She calls him in
for lunch from his work in the garden.
He says, *You didn't have to make
anything*, then notices what it is
and remembers too, and smiles,
and pulls her to him and knows
he never wants to let her go.

Norman's Surprise

When they come home from a drive,
Norman is clearly excited about something.
Sara wonders if a new poem is running
through his head. Now, in this beautiful home
they share, he has his office set up upstairs
and can write more easily.

She still has trouble with stairs so he took
photos for her to look at whenever she wants.
A queen sized bed with a dark green spread
and dresser fill one room for the boy and his wife.

Norman's office is in the second bedroom.
His computer, router, printers
and file cabinets plus a cot
for the boy's young son fill that room.
A bathroom next to a storage room for extras
is at the end.

Sara has her laptop online
downstairs and works on the purple sofa
they unanimously agreed was perfect
when spotted online then checked out
in the store for quality by Norman.

Once inside the front door Norman covers her eyes,
walks her through the room, turns her around
and seats her in a chair with arms and a foot rest.
A new piece of furniture?

It's your own power chair, he tells her.
Now you can get around inside
and out even on bad days.
She pulls him down for a kiss.

Protection

The doctor's office calls a week later.
Her antibodies have slipped since
the last testing and he recommends
the booster. Norman schedules
one for her and one for himself.
Being over fifty he's eligible
and most of all wants one to protect
her as well as possible, too.

Like with the original vaccinations
she has a week of headaches,
but he gets away with a sore arm.
He realizes nothing can fully keep them safe,
but he can do his best by trying.

When the headaches lift, their desire
for each other increased by the break
during the worst of them, she barely
gives him time to get his trousers off
before she's pulling him into her.

Sara's Fear

Gasping for breath,
heart pounding, Sara jerks
awake from a nightmare.
Covid still visits her unpredictably.
Not covid as it first hit her,
but the panic still roams free
in her mind. Her doctor tells her
it's post traumatic syndrome,
common in his patients
who had it as bad as she did.

She feels guilty. Yes, it was bad enough
but not like two fellow artists
who caught it visiting Manhattan
back when it first hit.
Before vaccinations.
Before boosters.
Back when the President was calling it
just a bad flu on t.v.
Back when anti maskers
rallied to not cover their faces.

Pans banged out windows
thanking health care workers
with no time to go home.
Cooler trucks were brought in
when the morgues were full.
Her one friend had to be intubated
and died not long after. The other
survived after supplementary oxygen,
but with lungs permanently damaged.

Yes, Sara is weak, but lucky.
She sometimes fears the weakness
will never pass, but she has Norman
to care about her now.

Sensing her restlessness he's already
sitting up in bed, arms around her,
telling her she's okay, knowing well
the needs that nightmares bring out.

Norman Wasn't Ready

Norman wasn't ready,
wasn't sure he ever would be,
couldn't imagine how the boy
could ever forgive him, how he
could feel anything but self-hatred,
soul-rending shame,
every bit as bad as his father.
The hit, the abandonment, the years
of nothing but sending money,
watching from afar, listening
to updates from Sara.
He never knew that Sara
had protected his reputation as well,
made up stories to excuse him,
continued to defend him even
when the boy knew the truth.

Norman cried right away,
uncontrolled, blubbering tears,
blurting out apology after apology.
He struggled to accept the boy's
forgiveness, to forgive himself,
until the boy said,
You've brought her back to joy.
Nothing matters as much as that.
At last, he understood.

When the Boy Came

When the boy came downstairs
the morning after he arrived
he found Norman in the kitchen,
coffee ready, two printer
paper boxes in front of him,
stuffed with envelopes, one a week
for all the years he'd been gone.
Eyes already full of tears,
he said, *I don't expect you*
to read them all today.
Hell, you don't have to read them at all.
Mostly they say I'm sorry.

Norman Remembers

Norman remembers the boy's fascination
with leaves and stars and dead things,
how he might *climb to them, reach them, travel*
to where they were and bring them back.

He remembers a day at the beach
and how he kept staring at the horizon,
saying, *It's not that far. I think*
We could make it, and I could see what's there.

He remembers his endless curiosity,
his wanting to talk about everything:
light and dark, near and far,
birth and death, the endless in between.

He remembers what once loomed so large
it blocked sight of everything else
but now has become just a shadow
in the distant background of every scene
he remembers.

Perspective

Sara remembers how bad it was
before vaccinations. People dying
with tubes down their throats
no family to hold their hands,
tell them goodbye. She barely went
anywhere that first year, shopped
for food, art supplies, even clothes
now and then using the internet.

Then there was toilet paper hoarding,
Often none to be found on the shelf . . .
what if I'm quarantined and run out.
Next came chicken. Sales of canned meat
went up. Masks were required to get
into most stores. Eat-in restaurants and shops
closed for lack of business.

The anti-maskers still refused wearing them.
Two of her favorite older collectors
were taken down by Covid, other people
she knew, as well. She remembered stories passed
from her grandmother about the Spanish flu,
a little girl during that time.
People were dying all over town, the doctor
going house to house with nothing much
he could do.

When Sara gets down now and is feeling bad
she reminds herself to be grateful she's alive,
not in a cold room somewhere,
unable to breathe without help,
a double masked, double gowned
passing nurse trying to hold back her tears,
and more than anything that she's not alone,
that the man she loves
and their son still live.

Alive and Growing

The first thing Norman wanted
in the new house was an herb garden.
He built 3-foot-high boxes
around the patio just outside
the kitchen door, leaving
an opening wide enough
for Sara's chair. He filled
the bottoms with gravel, followed
by a thick layer of shredded
palm bark, then a mix
of peat and loam. He planted
dill, German thyme, oregano,
garlic chives, sage, parsley,
basil, and rosemary, lots
of rosemary, which he liked
to run his hands through
anytime he went outside.
He saved one container
for nothing but mint, keeping
it separate from all the rest
so it wouldn't take over,
and one large box he kept
empty so Sara could choose
whatever annuals she wanted
for any time of year.
The boy helped with everything.
He wanted them to always
have fresh herbs for cooking.
He wanted them to enjoy

the smell such plants bestowed.
Mostly, he wanted them to be surrounded
by things alive and growing.

Sara's Hair

Sara's hair hits past her shoulders. She's been pulling it back
with a clasp so it's out of her face and doesn't look
so dirty when she's not able to wash it.

With Norman here she's cleaner than since she got sick.
Often he puts it into a plait down her back. When they make
love she likes to have him unplait it, at least between
the first and second times. No time usually to wait
before the first time. They're too eager. She wants
it to fall down and touch him when she's on top.

Norman Gets to Know His Son

The boy comes three weekends
in a row. Sara creates ways
for him and Norman to be alone.
He is everything Norman
could ever want him to be,
gentle, thoughtful, smart,
creative, fearless, ethical,
even in the face of self-interest,
everything Sara was,
everything Sara made Norman
want to be.

The Boy

Sara knew he was no longer
a boy, called him by his proper name
when talking to him or referring
to him to others. The same with Norman.
John had never been able to do that.
Maybe it was because of who he was
to them and how he represented
what they had produced together.
He would always be their boy,
even when his hair was gray as theirs was.
The boy worked in beach erosion,
needed everywhere now the oceans were rising.
Collins Avenue, just past the beach
in Miami Beach, where the models
and the rich hung out, flooded in storms
regularly now. Daytona Beach used to be
massive, now was a shell of itself.
All of this from the boy. He was based
north in the state but traveled and told Sara.
Now he would be telling Norman, too.
Sara liked to think of herself at times
trying to hold back her own tides,
the many times of despair when Norman
first left, the initial sweep of emotion when
she came near him, now feeling
safe enough to fully flow free again.

The Call

The boy calls Sara after his weekends
with Norman. They hadn't had time to talk much.

I always felt a piece of myself was missing,
he tells Sara. I don't feel that anymore.
I loved John and he was good to us
but I always wondered about my real father.
Now I know. The letters he gave me
tell me how torn he was about leaving us.

The boy had been ten when John moved in.
Before that, lumps of money would arrive sporadically
that Sara knew had to have come from Norman
but no notes ever came with the bank signed checks.
Her paintings were just beginning to sell
and the money was welcome so she never
pushed finding out more.

The five year anniversary of John's death
is next week, the boy reminds her.
She didn't need reminding. She had wondered
what Norman would feel if she asked him
to drive her to the cremation site
to toss some roses.

She needed to ask him soon but she
didn't want to cause a problem either.
Norman was always the one she loved.
She hopes he knows that by now.

Gratitude

Norman has always been amazed by Sara,
her courage, optimism, determination,
openness to every opportunity,
her body, of course, but also her laugh,
her smile, the depth of her thinking,
how she never gives up, never gets down,
and always cares more for others than herself.

Now, as he goes with her and the boy
to place flowers at the vault that holds
the ashes of a man who was kind to her,
who filled in when Norman was not enough,
whom she cared for but admits
she never fully loved, he finds himself
wanting to say, *Thank you.*

BETTER

Unplanned

She hadn't planned it
but suddenly her brush started
moving across the largest canvas.
Norman, in gradated shades of blue
holding the boy, painted in purple,
full grown, wearing a blue loincloth.

He lay sprawled in Norman's arms,
one arm dangling, head cocked,
as if Norman was carrying him,
their boy, their son,
back where he belonged.

Wildflowers covered Norman's feet.
Golden wings grew out of his back.
The pink of a sunrise covered
the canvas behind them. Their eyes
were identical, both looking out
of the canvas at someone looking in.
Sara felt that someone was her
and she was part of the painting
even though not in it.

She kept the painting turned
to the wall when Norman was close,
secretive when he asked
what she was working on...
nothing special right now.

She had already decided it
would be her gift to Norman
when she finished, never to be sold,
like the one in the bedroom.
She already knew he would like it.

Norman Comes In

Norman comes in from the yard
tired. He was up a lot last night
caring for Sara. She asks
if he'd like to rest. He says
Maybe I should. She makes a fuss,
removing his shoes, stacking pillows,
getting a blanket from the closet.
It feels good to her.
She checks on him repeatedly,
lingers at times, just watching,
growing more in love. After an hour
she wakes him with her hand,
then her mouth. He is ready
within moments, tries to rise
but she makes him lie still
until he can't wait any longer
then let's him finish inside her.
They fall asleep again
each holding tightly to the other.

Sara's Spaces

Sara remembers when she felt
an empty space surrounding her.
She knew that space was Norman,
that she needed to pull herself
out of the orbit they circled in tandem for years.

She told herself if she ran into him
on the street his eyes would go opaque
at the sight of her, sunglasses
of forgetfulness drawn down
low over his face.

Despite only glimpses of him
in years he had always been a part of her
that had to be amputated for her sanity.

She never could give away Norman's old shirt,
though, wearing it sometimes, pretending
his arms were still in it, around her.

How different things are now.
She hopes she's not feverish again,
having a Covid induced dream
that never could come true.

Flannel

On cool days, Norman still wears flannel
just a part of who he is, always has been,
having grown up on farms, hiking,
the grunge era, and one of the better parts,
durable, reliable, comfortable, warm.
Sara calls him her personal lumberjack,
loves to rub his arms, loves
how soft it is, loves to press
her face into the material.

Some mornings she'll go to his closet,
pick one out for herself, put it on
with nothing else and go to find him.

Time Travel

Sara finds her thoughts
traveling back to her first days
living at Green Street,
belly dancing in the window,
picking up nameless men at bars,
acting like the *little whore* Grandpa
always called her, hands roaming
her childhood body.

Then came Norman.
Then came love.

Even after he left out of fear
he might hurt the boy
like his father had hurt him,
she was changed.

No more men from bars.
The dancing more discreet.

He had left his mark on her
and now, back in her life for good,
her heart is filled with gratitude.
Her Norman. Where he should be.

Shadows of a Different Sort

Sara tells Norman she wants him to drive
her by Green Street, where their love started
so many years ago. She could have gone
many times over the years but avoided it . . .
the idea of it felt like walking on broken glass.
She had stayed there when John first moved in
but suddenly Norman was everywhere.

He was in bed when they made love.
She would begin to open the closet
or drawers and see his clothes there.
When she put dishes away she found herself
arranging them the way Norman would.
John had a good heart and she wanted
a male figure around for the boy so she
suggested they move to another place
a few miles away. Just said she was
in the mood for a change.

They park across the street
from the old apartment. Whoever lives
there now is home – Sara sees shadows
move across the window. For a minute
she feels she's in her body but up there
as well, the young Norman and Sara
going about their day.

She feels she's come full circle,
a place inside she never thought
she would find again. She takes Norman's hand
and sees he feels it, too. The part of the old
Norman that had to run has run right back
to her, healed.

Ornithology

Norman keeps a list of birds.
Starts fresh every month.
Last month he had 60.
It's Florida.
He says on Roanoke he rarely
had more than half that many
unless he went out looking for them.

He asks Sara to go bird watching
with him. She laughs at first,
then realizes he is serious.
She says, *I couldn't possibly*
manage to go very far.
I just can't walk that long.
He says, *Don't worry I'm prepared for that.*

One morning they pack a lunch,
head out early. Norman has binoculars
and bird books ready on the console.
Thirty minutes later he turns
down a one-way road crossing
a wide, flat lake with patches
of marsh and trees. He points
a little way in, and says,
Spoonbills and Ibises.
She looks through the glasses
and watches, amazed for several minutes.
They continue driving slowly,
stopping often, seeing Osprey
and Eagles, Storks and Egrets,
Plovers and Terns,
a Peregrine Falcon, and
Black-Crowned Night Herons,
nearly a hundred species in all,
including Sara's favorite,
an Eastern Kingfisher that seems
to follow them most of the way,
chittering as if to her, and darting
in and out of lakewater and canal.

After seven miles they find a place
to lay out a blanket and eat.
Sara naps afterward,
and then again on the drive home.
For the next week Sara
paints nothing but birds,
and after that
almost all her women have wings.

Loosening Up

Sara notices that gradually
Norman's clothes don't look straight
out of a department store, unlike when
they were together before.

His casual shirts are folded looser,
his hanging clothes are no longer
color coordinated, the spaces
between them are becoming uneven.

The kitchen cabinets are still organized,
the table set just so but if the glasses
don't match it doesn't bother him.

For the first time she can see clearly
how tight his self control must have been.
The organization had helped him
keep scary feelings under cover.
She's glad when she sees a pair
of his pants on the floor, not immediately
tossed into the hamper.

Norman Never Worked Out

Norman never worked out,
never seemed to need to,
still long and lean,
muscles still subtly defined,
not the frightening bulge
of those obsessed with weights
but nonetheless pleasing to look at.
One day he washes the car
in nothing but a pair of shorts,
everything wet and rippling
as he moves, and his prodigious
size impossible to hide.
Sarah watches him from inside,
grows wetter by the minute,
thinks of calling him in,
decides to leave him be,
just keep watching
and take care of things herself.

Resolutions

Sara thinks of early times,
when he first left, how
she thought about chasing him
down, assuring him things
would be okay if he came back.

She even got as far as his street once
before he moved away, before making
the decision to live with John
but stopped herself. He would
come back only if he chose to.

She resolved never to go that far
with her wishes for impossible things
again, never to try to see him,
never to think of how things used to be.

Now with him beside her, holding
her hand, she resolves to stop
making resolutions about things
when she has no idea how they
will resolve in the end.

Better

There was no miracle making
everything suddenly go right.
Things still went wrong,
the hammer hitting the back
of the thumb, the trash bag
spilling down the hallway,
the inability to sleep, rude people,
nightmares, intolerance, anxiety,
disagreements, all the everyday disasters
that could befall anyone
and cause his father to rise up
inside him, leading
to anger, frustration,
even a violent response.
The difference is that now
when something goes wrong
Norman thinks first of Sara
and how she needs him
and whether she's okay
and how he can make it better.

The Family

He thought they should know her
as something other than sick,
so when she told him the boy
was bringing his family for a visit,
he framed and hung every painting
she would let him to show them
what she still could do.
He did all he could to keep her well,
rested, energized for the day.
Then spent the day making sure
she didn't over exert herself,
attending to needs
before they were even spoken.
He stayed so busy that he never
even recognized his own fear.
And when they left and the little one,
his own grandson, hugged him,
and told him, *Thank you,*
Grandpa, for loving Grandma,
any fear that had been there
completely melted away.

He Liked Her

Instantly.
How could he not?
The hug she greeted him with
was as warm and accepting
as any he'd ever gotten
from even his longest friends,
better than he'd gotten from most.
And everything about her
reminded him of Sara,
the way she looked, moved,
spoke, treated everything
with a gentle strength
and an open mind,
allowing everything,
including her son,
the joy of being,
the exhilaration of self discovery.
None of that surprised him.
He imagined the boy wise enough
To know good when he saw it,
careful enough to keep it close
to him when given the chance.

Helping Out

Sara's former renter calls...
can Sara help?
One of her friends has long term covid
like Sara does and her husband
is threatening to leave if she doesn't
shape up and get over this nonsense.

The woman cries on the phone
with Sara for an hour.
Nobody in her family believes her.
She's lazy.
She's doing this to get out
of giving dinner parties.
She just doesn't want to drive the kids.

Sara's heard it all from the other man.
Just different details.
The woman is stuck,
no Norman to help her out.

She tells her they'll talk again,
to ignore what he says.
Maybe Norman can bring her over
one day so they can meet.
Perhaps a referral to her specialist
who's good at dealing with men
like her husband and Sara's last man.
Right now she's seeing her old
internist who's almost useless.

When she hangs up
she holds Norman extra close.
For better or worse, she whispers,
thinks he doesn't hear her, but he does
and his heart fills.

Legacy

After seeing how Sara's face lit up
on the bird-watching motor trail,
Norman knew he needed more
winged things in the backyard
to be a part of her life every day.
He planted a butterfly bush
in one corner, put a bird bath
in the center surrounded
by Black-Eyed Susans, Columbine,
Tickseed, Bee Balm, Echinacea,
and hung a feeder nearby,
triple silo for more variety,
thistle for finches, sunflower
seeds for larger birds,
millet mixed with mealworms
for the rest. She spent part
of every day sitting on the patio
or looking out the kitchen window
to see what would come,
finches and sparrows,
titmice and vireos,
chickadees and nuthatches.
In the other corner he planted
a hornbeam, called it Sara's tree.
When she asked him why,
noting it lacked the usual romance
of camelia, magnolia, wisteria,
he said, *Because it reminds me*
of you. It's the toughest
tree I know. It will be here
when your grandchildren have grandchildren.

Sara's Fears Re-emerge

After a number of better days
Sara is in bed again dizzy and weak.
When Norman comes to check on her,
tears flow.

What if I don't get better, she cries.
Will you stop loving me?

You've been better already, he tells her.
You will be again.
And I'll be here either way.

Sara knows part of her fear is a tiny bit
of grandfather still inside, telling her
that her parents would give her away.

The time has long come to let grandfather
go completely, she tells herself.
In sickness and in health, Norman whispers.
She burrows into Norman's arms.

Norman Begins to Imagine a Happy Ending

For years, he looked mostly backwards,
into darkness, despair, anger,
and his poems showed it, tackling
abuse, abandonment, lost hope,
self-loathing. Even with students,
he insisted on the old ways,
writing only on paper,
never using technology
until the poem was done.
Now he writes everywhere,
mostly talks into his own phone
and transcribes later. And his subjects?
Birds and herbs, sunrises and beaches,
hope, love, redemption.
He never thought he could deserve it,
never really believed
it happened for anyone, but lately
he has fallen in love with happy endings.

Don't Wanna Talk About It

Norman has gone for groceries.
Even though she's now boosted
and wears a mask around others
he doesn't want the risk
of taking her to crowded public places.
Their Florida governor is taking away
more and more precautions,
backing demands of the pro-choicers
when it comes to vaccinations
and masks. Covid still lurks
and even a mild case can take you down,
as Sara has learned, but she rarely
sees a mask now.

She listens to music while he's gone.
Rod Stewart digs deep inside.
I don't wanna talk about it
how you broke my heart...
She remembers listening to this one
time after time when Norman first left.
He's back now and she knows (mostly)
he won't leave, but the old sadness
flows through her again.
Songs can do that. They dig in
and everything past comes alive
as if it just happened.

Conflict Resolution

They have a disagreement.
Voices are raised,
harsh words exchanged.
They go to bed angry.
She snuggles in anyway.
He holds her anyway.
Lying together warmth
passes between them.
He decides he was just tired,
took things the wrong way.
She decides she didn't feel good,
said things the wrong way.
They both say *I'm sorry*
at the same time.

Once Sara Saw...

funerals embedded
in every christening,
a divorce judge lurking
outside every wedding.
And yet he challenged her.
She walked the plank over
turbulent dream waters,
sliced her feet at its edges nightly.

After he left, she wanted to sit
by the sea nightly, forget
how the moon changed color
whenever he came inside her,

but back now, Norman bandages
her wounds, tosses out her long
litany of doubt. Her feet send
down roots, not unlike those
of a flower just sprung from seed,
uncertain it can bear the strength
of the morning sun until he holds her.

Norman Wakes at 2 A.M.

Norman wakes at 2 A.M.,
crying, not from a nightmare.
He hasn't had one of those
for weeks, longer than he has ever
gone without one before.
He walks quietly to the bathroom,
closes the door to avoid
waking Sara. He has had
such a pleasant dream
that it woke him with tears of joy.
He stays a few minutes
to quiet himself again.
When he returns to bed,
Sara is gone. He searches
and finally finds her in the kitchen,
naked, refrigerator door open,
eating plums from a bowl,
juices dripping her off her chin.
He clears his throat so not
to scare her. She turns, beautiful
and innocent in the dim light.
He bends forward to lick
the juice from her breasts and belly,
begins crying again.
He had given up all hope
of being happy, but now he is.

Two Way

Sara wakes from a nap
to find Norman sitting beside her
a cup of tea in each hand.
He sets them down
to help her sit up,
then hands her one
and takes a sip from the other.
What would I do without you,
she says. He replies,
I've been thinking about that.
I have something important
to tell you.

Sara's heart beats faster.
He can't handle it anymore,
is her first thought.
He's leaving.

You worry that I do too much,
but you need to know that I know
you would have gotten yourself out.
It would have just taken more time.
And you need to know you saved me.
If you hadn't gotten the nerve
to make that call, let me know
how sick and trapped you were
I would still be living on my island
alone. I would have grown old alone,
with the woman I still loved
somewhere else, not knowing
I still loved her because I was too
afraid to tell her so, never knowing
how my son was doing,
Eventually I would have died alone.
You gave me back my life.
You gave me the chance to change it,
to make it something worthwhile.
Your courage brought me back.

We help each other, he finishes.
You need to know that.
Sick or well, you're my angel.

The room is blurred by her tears.

Norman Has a Reading

Norman has a reading at a college
three hours away. He'll be gone
most of the day. It will be the longest
they've been apart since he came to help her.
She can't help but worry
he'll go home with someone
younger, healthier, less complicated,
that he won't come back,
but he texts every half hour.
Love you.
Still Love you.
Love you even more.
Even when he would have been reading
he somehow must have paused to text,
Wish I were with you.
And then, *Heading back soon.*
Leaving now.
Love you more than yesterday.
He knows it seems a little silly
but he means every word.
She knows it too.

Norman at the Reading

Sara's strong enough to get food
and the chair helps a lot so she insists
Norman keep his reading date
three hours away. They've scattered
seating for social distancing
and require masks. He's vaccinated
but must keep his health for Sara's sake.

The reading means more sales
of his latest book. He can decide
about getting back to teaching later.

He recognizes the woman up front
from the time after Sara. She came
to his readings then, and took him
home, more than once.
From the way she's dressed- nipples
tight against a fitted top, one leg
crossed and swinging provocatively,
it's clear she's expecting a repeat tonight.
In the past he wouldn't have hesitated.
She's gorgeous and knows how
to push his buttons in bed.

Now? No desire rushes through him.
When she approaches him, he's gentle,
says it's good to see her again,
but he has somewhere he has to go.

He can hardly wait to get back to Sara.

A View of Blue

Sara rarely tries to climb
the stairs to Norman's office.
Doing so is always a strain
and presents the inherent hazard
of a fall with long term consequences.
But on one particularly bad day
neither the green of the backyard
nor the street scene from her studio
seems enough. So Norman
lifts her in his arms
and carries her up the stairs
to the recliner in his office
aimed perfectly to frame
an endless perspective of blue sky,
white wisps of cloud,
the occasional bird in flight.
And she sits for hours
with Norman bringing her tea,
reading her poetry, the view
of blue the best medicine
she has had in years.

Sara Talks to the Stars

Sara's awake while Norman sleeps.
Her illness can cause exhaustion
and insomnia in the same day.
She thinks of waking him,
his favorite way,
her hands between his legs,
or maybe just snuggling up to him.
She thinks of how much
he has done lately
and decides to let him rest,
rises quietly instead,
slips on her gown,
and heads through the kitchen
into the back yard.

It's a warm, clear night,
and the stars are out.
She talks to them,
voices her worries
about letting him down,
about not having the strength
to be an equal partner,
about being too fragile,
that she might break,
fall apart, collapse completely.
She worries her love won't be enough,
that she has little else to offer.
Tonight she worries most
that he doesn't understand
how thankful she is.

The stars remain,
far away,
twinkling above,
sure in their spot in the heavens,
bigger than her,
bigger than all her worries.

She goes inside
to make sure he knows.

Sara's Realization

Sara sits in a lawn chair
while Norman trims the hedges
out back. Two blackbirds squabble
over the bird feeder.

Unexpectedly, a noise. The man
Norman rescued her from
walks into the back yard
carrying a cardboard box.

Found your crap all over
my house, he says. *Got*
your address from a realtor friend.
He tosses the box
at Sara's feet. A tee shirt,
underpants, leggings, paint brushes
she thought had been misplaced.

Norman hasn't heard him
over the roar of the motor.

Knocked but nobody came,
he adds. *Figured you were*
too lazy to come to the door.
He nods his head at Norman,
I see you have somebody else
to be your slave now, pretending
to be oh so helpless.

Sara knew he wasn't the only person
who judged her. Others did
when she went by in her chair.
Whispers. Addressing comments
over her head to Norman
as if she was the village idiot.

Before she can reply, he turns
and strides out of the yard.
She lets him go.

She comes to a new realization.
She thought she was strong when Norman left,
again when John died, not letting
anything take her down like her grandfather
did, but now, with Norman so kind,
she realizes she had not been as strong
as she thought. When Covid was over
and she couldn't infect him, she could have called
the boy, asked him to move her into a long stay motel
with kitchenette until her renters moved.

She could have afforded someone
to bring meals, drive her to the doctor.
She could have left as soon as the man
started getting nasty even before Covid
but blamed it on no place to go.

Norman had saved her in more ways
than bringing her out. He saved her
by loving her as she was, vulnerable.
Being vulnerable was her greatest fear.
She suddenly could see that clearly.
He let her see that she still had the last
remnants of grandfather's days inside her,
too easily acquiescing to the man's abuse.

Like the Phoenix, a new Sara
was emerging now from the ash.
When Norman shuts down the trimmer
and walks over to her, she throws
her arms around him and says,
Thank you. He looks perplexed
but smiles and hugs her, happy
for anything she feels he has given her.

CONSUMMATION

As If

As if the way he loved her body
wasn't enough,
as if the memories of all she had done for him
weren't enough,
as if the beauty with which she saw the world and portrayed it on
canvas
wasn't enough,
as if her courage and strength surviving everything life had thrown at
her
weren't enough,
even her voice was the perfect lure for Norman's love,
deep and sultry to begin with,
made breathy and warm by illness,
at times frail,
at times almost a whisper,
but always more than anything,
the most sincere thing he had ever heard.

It was almost unfair the way it called to him.
He knew he would always answer,
sometimes even before she spoke.
Like on the day the wind before a storm
caught her in the backyard
and she stood amidst a shower of petals,
beauty among beauty, and caught his eye.
She might have said *Come join me*,
but he was already there,
needing no words to know what to do.

For Sara, Again

he
makes coffee every morning
breakfast
empties the trash
opens windows
folds clothes
mows
plants a garden
weeds
picks parsley, rosemary, basil,
vacuums,
cooks,
puts away dishes,
organizes cabinets,
shows her house wren, cosmos, autumn joy
remains different
stays patient
listens
lingers
lets go
of everything but her

Doing More

Each day she can do a little more
as long as she paces herself.
The old energy is beginning to flow
through her body again and Norman
is there if she needs a day in bed
to make up for any overdoing.

For times she wants to do more
she uses the power chair
to go outside and enjoy the fresh air
before she has to sleep again.
He fastens a 'learners permit' tag
on the back, giving them both a laugh.

Her doctor had told her there was no way
to exercise her way out of long term Covid.
Days at the gym or squats at home
weren't the solution, that she needs
to give her body time to heal itself,
if it will, so she does what she can,
feels no judgment from Norman,
unlike the last man,
and continues to hope.

Taking Inventory

The last thing he does every night,
a sort of prayer, he thinks,
reflecting on the day's events,
things he said, did,
choices he made. Looking
for anything he might regret,
lost patience or opportunity,
cross word, failure to help.
He writes it down.
Then below it a resolution
for how he can correct it
the next day.
Sara teases him playfully,
says, *The counting Norman
isn't completely gone.*
He says, *I never believed
in regret. Undoing one thing
would undo them all.
Yet I've lived with regret
my whole life, regret
for losing control, once,
for not being with you,
and for missing out
on being a father.
I don't want to risk
missing out again.*

Wild Sara Returns

Wild Sara returns,
now and then,
hair down,
hips writhing ecstatically,
hands aching to paint
anything, everything,
willing to try it all,
fears, inhibitions, concerns
abandoned, as if
nothing is beyond her,
moments when she feels
less fragile, less damaged,
more frequent now,
with Norman back.
He makes her feel
if not completely healed,
at least less
than completely broken.

Sara Knows

Sara can see when Norman tenses,
knows he's reliving the beatings.
He doesn't run now, can breathe,
focus on her, write a poem
and ease back into the moment.
Before, running was the only option he saw.
She understands, still shakes
when older men try to push her too hard,
has the occasional urge to go to her back
with an attractive man she passes.
Always the bad ones, it turns out.
Except for Norman her judgment
in men is still impaired.

She pulls out her paintbrush, grateful
for gifts life brings when least expected.

Consummation

Sara woke,
showered,
had breakfast on the patio,
made love,
showered again,
washed the sheets,
loaded the dishwasher,
had a late lunch at a café,
came home,
napped,
made love again,
painted,
called the boy,
let Norman make salads for dinner,
had wine on the patio,
showered a third time,
and fell asleep
with Norman holding her.

It was the most complete day
she had had in years.

The Unveiling

Sara never thought size mattered.
More a question of technique, creativity, art.
But when she saw this one,
so big it took her breath away,
made her imagination run wild,
she decided she had to have it,
let Norman bring it to her,
and once she touched it, she knew
exactly what to do with it.

She got started right away,
but kept her progress concealed
from Norman's eyes,
and when he asked about it,
she said she was just playing with it,
nothing serious, though she worked at it
feverishly, up early and late,
sometimes collapsing in between.

When ready, she waited until Norman
and the boy could be there together,
and uncovered it in front of them both.
Norman was clearly moved,
tears falling over a constant smile.
The boy stood studious, taking it
all in piece by piece, finally
seemed at ease, hugged his father.

The entire canvas was covered
with things alive and growing,
things with wings, all their favorites,
kingfishers and herons, rosemary
and mint, the hornbeam,
and in the center, larger than life,
painted in purples and blues,
Norman carried the boy,
as he had carried Sara
many times before. They both looked out
at whoever was looking in.
They both knew it was Sara.

Feeling Like Home

Six months in the house
and they've made it theirs.
Sara's winged women are scattered
throughout the rooms until she sells
all but her two favorites.
Norman's abstract with the purple breasted
woman has a permanent place
in the bedroom. She finally tells him
who it is. He replies that he always knew.
Norman is almost through with his next book,
manuscript stacked neatly beside his desk.

The question hangs in the air, but neither
wants to be first to say it.
Finally, Sara tells Norman she wants
to live out her life with him but is terrified
of marriage. She's seen it affect too many
relationships badly. He tells her that
marry or not is fine with him.
He wants the same thing she does.

Sara says one of her former renters
used to have ceremonies for gay couples
before marriage was legal, that it might
be nice to have the boy and his family come
and do something like that in the backyard.
They can make their own pledges,
let the boy see this was forever.

Norman loves the idea, especially
the scent of their herbs filling the air around them.

Vows

Neither knew what the other would say.
They only promised to keep it simple.

Sara had ordered a purple dress online,
keeping it out of Norman's sight.
Long, it draped her slender figure
as she hoped it would. The light in his eyes
when she stepped into the yard
told her it was doing its magic.

He took her arm and they walked
together to the space they had chosen.
Standing with him, the sun
seemed brighter, the flowers fuller.
Her heart pounded with excitement,
with the joy of this moment.

She had rehearsed so many things
she wanted to say, but finally decided
to go with what came out.
The words flowed so easily
she could barely remember
all that she said until...

I'm blessed that you returned to me.
You are the man I've always loved
and always will love.

He looked deep into her eyes,
tears slowly forming, mouth
almost unable to move.
His reply was perfect.

Every day of my life with you
has been better than any day without you.
You've given me the life
I never thought I could have.
But there are still skies I haven't seen with you,
still mornings I haven't risen with you,
still birds I haven't listened to with you,
still nights we haven't filled with love.
I want to share them all with you.

They kissed slowly then turned
to embrace their family, a new life
already building beneath their feet.

Their Time Away

Norman had the car packed
early the next morning
after the ceremony.
The boy and his family had driven home
after a dinner cooked by Norman
and served on the patio.

They found a place on the Gulf
near a huge drive-through bird sanctuary.
No steps in. First floor bedroom.
He rented a chair for the week.
Too hard to transport hers. Even though
she no longer uses it as much, he knows
she still needs it.

The birds are beautiful. Egrets, herons,
a surprise visit by an anhinga, spreading
its silver wings to dry after swimming. Usually
they don't stray far from the Everglades.
Sunsets over the Gulf every evening
are followed by lovemaking even more intense
than at the beginning, if that is possible.

She imagines them at eighty, sitting somewhere
holding hands, looking up at the sky together.
She imagines their ashes merging even after
their time on the planet is gone.

Norman in the Rear View

A quiet moment, mind wandering,
and there he is, out of nowhere,
narrowed eyes, gritted teeth,
the monster he thought gone forever,
the past he feared that never happened,
exactly, that he thought he'd avoided by leaving,
so much like his father that he nearly recoils,
nearly lashes out, instead,
just sits transfixed until he feels
her hand reach and touch his thigh.
Without a word, it all dissolves.
He knows it will always be there.
He also knows so will she.
He simply says, *I love you.*

Sara's Dream

Norman has been gone
to his workshop for a week now.
He's become a planet
 in the constellation of rising stars.
Women swoon when he shares
his poems, beg him for kisses,
passion that he gives only to Sara.

The house tilts. Trees
turn upside down. Sara was alone
many times before Norman but
he's changed her compass readings.
Her true north shifts south.

She dreams that night he comes to her,
bearing platters of luminescents
from the sea, surrounded by starfish.
Their ghostly shapes merge all night.

Too soon dawn. He leaves her
tingling with an odd longing to rush
to the sea and swim to him.
If only she could, but walking is barely
possible with her illness.

When he arrives home he holds out
a silver chain with a hand-crafted starfish
 hanging from it. She pinches herself
to see if she's dreaming again
then draws him deep into their sea-driven
dive to her depths.

Settling In

Sara is planning an art showing,
a big one. They decide that Norman
will read poems inspired by each one,
already framed and hanging, too.

They've fallen into their vows
like shooting stars find their way
across the sky with no map.
She can't imagine loving anyone more.

Her body is stronger.
She still has to rest but believes
she'll always be all Norman wants
her to be, weak or strong.
To him, it's not what he loves about her.

He walks outside with a cup of tea.
They watch the sky turn pink
all around them. A blackbird sings.
He kisses with a promise of the night
yet to come.

Courage

Of all the things he ever thought he'd be,
a coward was the last. Always fast
to join in the fight, protect anyone
he saw mistreated out of some sense
of gallantry he clung to, some belief
in what was right, some desire
to make up for his own childhood, unafraid
of what might happen to him, but aware
that he feared the abuser could easily be him.
He knew now the cowardice he'd shown
by leaving, although he called it courage,
willingness to be alone rather than hurt
someone he loved. He knew too that he wasn't
ready then, but had the courage now
to face everything that was
and everything that might yet to be.

New Routine

She paints.
He writes.
They cook together,
shop together,
shower together,
talk nonstop.
At night,
almost every night,
sometimes in the morning,
sometimes after lunch,
sometimes in unexpected places,
they make love.

It all feels
ideal.
Her life
becomes the poem
she always wanted
him to write.
His poems
feature the life
he always wanted
to live.

AFTERWORDS

The Author Finds Norman

Before, the Sara in me spent her time
gallivanting in poems from man to man.
One night stands.
Over and over.
She never really wanted any of them
to stay in her bed after, would go
to theirs whenever possible.
No one could stay long enough
to hurt her, take her down like grandpa.

When Norman appeared,
something in Sara awakened.
She couldn't put a name to it
but she wanted more.
One night led to two
then to moving in together.

When he left, a psychic friend
said their souls were joined.
He would return.

I wondered if a part of you spoke
to me in the undercover of strange events,
called to my Sara in the darkness
of fiercest storms, the light
of falling stars during that absence.

Three books of Norman and Sara.
That's what it took until things settled.
Settled for me, too, since that Sara
part of me had grieved for him.

The Author Finds Sara

Before, Norman's only redemption
was giving back the natural way,
a corpse in the ground.
Sara gave him a reason to change,
hope that love could be enough.

When at first it wasn't,
he did all he knew how to do
to save those he loved,
all he had ever been taught.
He ran and thought to stay that way,
but you saw more,
Sara's great passion unsatisfied,
Norman's core of goodness,
and reached out knowing the one thing
that would bring him back,
the code he lived by
that caused him to leave to begin with.

Once there, all other
motivations faded
to insignificance, all other
possibilities froze in time.
All he needed was her open hand,
and the rest became inevitable.

Alter Egos

We whisper our secrets
through Norman and Sara,
things you would never tell me
as me, but the truth lies bare
whenever they meet.

I know we've made love
in make believe places
but to tell you that it
sometimes seems like we
really did would scare you,
send you hiding
in dark corners behind
bird faced women, flapping
their wings to fly you away.

We keep our masks on,
let Norman and Sara loose
to add forbidden spice
to routined lives.
We paint poems into hidden
chambers to be read only later
by ardent seekers, glad to find
words that speak loudly about
relationships that, even unspoken,
can still bring joy to the dying faces
of uprooted daisies.

The Authors Discuss Whose Name Should Go First

I know that I am not Norman.
You know that you are not Sara.
But there's a little piece
of each of them in each of us
that shows us how to be
kinder, love stronger, live better.
And Norman would never put himself
before Sara. Call it chivalry.
Call it appreciation. Call it respect.
Call it simply alphabetical, but let's leave it
by Pris Campbell and Scott Owens.

A Letter to the Other Author

Dear Scott,

Sara tells me she's found her peace reuniting with Norman.

I thought for a long time it would never happen, especially when Norman disappeared and, for so long, you indicated that you had no desire to wake him from his emotional slumber.

Ages back, I wrote you that if you didn't finally get around to replying to an email I sent I would write a poem about Norman and Sara marrying. You replied immediately. I think you knew I was kidding but didn't want to take the risk I might do it. (I wouldn't have).

Then one day, Sara wrote Norman again. She never had stopped loving him. As her emissary, I sent you the poem. At first Norman wrote back, turning away, then, inexplicably, in the next email, his face turned towards hers. His long time love for her finally was clear again. They kept writing and this book was born.

Now, I have no more ways to blackmail you, twist your arm, if you don't email. I see no obvious way to share our writing anymore now that our jobs as go-betweens for Sara and Norman are finally done. Maybe Sara can think of a way later. She's very clever.

You have been a poetic blessing in my life and I thank you. I thank Norman, too, for coming back home to us both.

Pris

For Now

We say we're done, again,
and so we are until one
or the other writes another,
and then the other responds
with yet another, and we're off
and running again, the way
climbing one hill always
exposes the next to climb,
and who can ever say *Stop*
until there's nothing more
to explore, nothing left
to see or be, until
life itself leaves
you no other option, at least
none that you know of.
And Sarah and Norman are not
in the ground yet and perhaps
never will be, and neither
are you nor I, and so
when we say we're done,
again, what we really mean
is at least for now.

AUTHOR BIOS

PRIS CAMPBELL

The poems of Pris Campbell have appeared in numerous journals and anthologies, including PoetsArtists, Nixes Mate, Rusty Truck, Bicycle Review, The Red Fez, Boxcar Poetry Review, and Outlaw Poetry. Nominated seven times for a Pushcart, the Small Press has published twelve collections of her poetry. She also writes short forms and took first place in the Marlene Mountain monoku contest and the Sanford Goldstein tanka competition in 2021 and second place in the 2022 Samurai tanka contest. A former Clinical Psychologist, sailor and bicyclist until sidelined by ME/CFS, a neuroimmune illness, in 1990, she makes her home with her husband in the Greater West Palm Beach, Florida.

SCOTT OWENS

Scott Owens is the author of 19 collections of poetry and recipient of awards from the Academy of American Poets, the Pushcart Prize Anthology, the Next Generation/ Indie Lit Awards, the NC Writers Network, the NC Poetry Society, and the Poetry Society of SC. His poems have been featured on The Writer's Almanac 8 times, and his articles about writing poetry have been used in Poet's Market 4 times. Owens holds degrees from Ohio University, UNC Charlotte, and UNC Greensboro. He is Professor of Poetry at Lenoir Rhyne University, and former editor of Wild Goose Poetry Review and Southern Poetry Review. He owns and operates Taste Full Beans Coffeehouse and Gallery and coordinates Poetry Hickory in Hickory, NC.